In the Bible, the word "heart" occurs 1,024 times. The heart is circulating blood through the body of humans and animals. Today, the heart is also the locus of whole psychological, intellectual, and moral life. The heart is an active center where the ideas and impressions are transformed into deeds. The heart is the center of individual's creative power in the form of consciousness.

A Brilliant Cardiologist And This
Crazy World

A Brilliant Cardiologist And This Crazy World

Nadia Russ

NeoPopRealism Press
www.neopoprealism.org

Language: English

A Brilliant Cardiologist and This Crazy World
Author: Nadia Russ

ISBN: 9781733867863

Printed in the USA
First published in the USA in 2023

All inquiry can be directed by email to
NeoPopRealism Press:
neopoprealism@protonmail.com

The NeoPopRealism Press' mission is to publish books that contribute in fundamental way to the art world and society.

CONTENT

INTRODUCTION

What is going on here, on this planet? Nothing much, everything is "as planned." The World Economic Forum is acquiring the God's divine powers. They also said that Jesus is the fake news and the new religion is here to unite all of humanity in worshiping the climate "science", eugenics, and techno-communism. They also promise to turn the people into gods (who will own nothing and will be happy). But let's find out what is really going on.

World Economic Forum ✓
@wef

Jesus is the original fake news.

11:23 PM · Nov 22, 2022 · Twitter Web App

Screenshot from Twitter: "Jesus is the original fake news."
https://yournews.com/2022/11/29/2462932/klaus-schwab-god-
is-dead-and-the-wef-is-acquiring/

Harari talking about WEF's success and its acquiring the God's
powers.
https://www.youtube.com/watch?v=N2kLBJN5MIQ

CHAPTER 1

THE ANCIENT WORLD HUMAN SACRIFICE AND THE MODERN MONSTERS

The ancient world was a very cruel place. Both animal and human sacrifice was a common thing, and most of the time it was performed in the context of making an offering to the gods. New research has found a lot of evidence that the Ancient Carthaginians practiced the human sacrifice. Children, mostly a few weeks old, were sacrificed at locations called the tophets. The sacrifice was also carried out by their neighbors, in Sicily, Malta, and

Sardinia.

The **Ancient Egyptians human sacrifice** was a type of sacrifices in which the pharaohs servants were killed so they continue to serve their died pharaohs in the afterlife.

The ancient Hawaiians believed that by sacrificing humans they could achieve a victory in their battles, gaining the favor of the god of war. Sacrifices were held in temples. The people used were captives, the chiefs from other tribes, who were hung upside down on wooden racks. The victim was beaten until his flesh became smooth. The ritual continued by eating his flesh either cooked or raw by the priest and the chief of the tribe.

A large number of ancient societies had the vitalistic conception of the heart as the center of courage and strength. This is why they loved to eat the hearts of their enemies hopping to acquire their power.

The Aztec and earlier Maya practiced sacrifice based on the notion of the heart as source of life. The Aztec sacrifices were symbolic and ritualistic acts accompanying feasts and festivals. This is how they were honoring the gods. The victims died in the center stage amid the splendor of dancing troupes, orchestras, costumes, and flower carpets. Aztec texts refer to human sacrifice as "the desire to be regarded as a god."

In the Inca empire, the heart was torn out when it still was beating. It resulted in a copious hemorrhage. The flowing blood was nourishment for the Sun.

The practice of human sacrifice was a very usual thing in ancient China, especially during the Shang Dynasty. The purpose was the political control and religious communication.

Human sacrifice in the Codex Magliabechiano, Folio 70. Heart-extraction was viewed as means of liberating the Istli and reuniting it with the Sun. The victim's transformed heart flies Sun-ward on a trail of blood (image from Wikipedia)

**Visual accounts of Aztec sacrificial practice are found in codices
and some Aztec statuary (image from Wikipedia)**

Isn't this fabulous that we live not in the cruel Ancient world? But wait! Even now, in 21st century, there are a lot of modern monsters, who enjoy torn out and eat the human hearts, saying figuratively. This world is filled with the negative and positive actions. One category of people is on a mission to destroy and they are proud of what they are doing. Another category of people is here to modestly fix the things. I would compare these people with the sun. If there is a shadow, there should be the shining sun. Darker the shadow, the sun is brighter.

Photo by Nadia Russ. Sunflowers, November 6, 2022, NYC

The modern monsters have developed the abnormalities of their hearts, which actually made them the monsters. They need a treatment. However, the regular cardiologists here would be powerless, despite their experience, knowledge of heart and a willing to help. These people need to fix their hearts another way. The corruption of human nature is taught in the Scripture and brought into connection with the heart, that is "hardened" (Exodus 4:21); "perverse" (Proverbs 11:20); "wicked" (Proverbs 26:23); "godless" (Job 36:13); "deceitful and desperately wicked" (Jeremiah 17:9 the King James Version). There were mentioned also the ways of the heart renewal. It is the removal of a "stony heart" (Ezekiel 11:19). The heart becomes "fixed" (Psalms 112:7) through "the fear" of the Lord (verse 1); it becomes "clean" (Psalms 51:10). On the "heart" the power of God is exercised for renewal (Jeremiah 31:33).

The last decades, and especially past few years, this planet experiences the wicked and hardened hearts plandemic. Typically it is spreading through the banknotes and with Stupidity Syndrome, which is very contagious. Stupidity Syndrome is a complex of symptoms indicating the undesirable trait of stupidity. While all people tend to be stupid without having it, the people with Stupidity Syndrome are inherently stupid. When persons get the large banknotes for their wrongdoings and at the same time having Stupidity Syndrome, these people becoming wickedly hardened and stupid every waking moment of their lives. There is no special treatment yet for this disease at the moment and the correct injection was not developed yet. This is why this planet now is like a rolling black rock. These people get injected with other things. The injections became the fashion trend, popular among athletes, celebrities, and the regular folks. They are necessity to prosper and save the planet. More injections, more success. It is like if your were wearing the Gucci clothes - all doors get automatically open for you. The CDC became the new political party and the new religion headquarters in the US with huge influence around the world.

The Stupidity Syndrome was in the US and worldwide for years already. In 2010, in Texas, a new variant, called "Amazing Stupidity Syndrome" suddenly appeared. But then, it did not reach its plandemic size yet. This is the report made by Jim Hightower from Truthout. He wrote it in December of 2010 : "... Another Texas politician has come down with the tragic disease known as "Amazing Stupidity Syndrome." A.S.S. attacks the lobe of the brain that controls one's ethical behavior, apparently causing the moral synapses in that region to go on the fritz, thus allowing the stupidity hormone to seep in and take charge. The main symptom is that afflicted legislators develop sticky fingers, causing them to double-bill for airline tickets, rooms at luxury resorts, lavish meals, etc."

Fortunately this disease cannot be asymptomatic and all infected should be placed into special quarantine facilities to stop the spread, up until the right medication would be developed and approved by the FDA. It would take probably a few years. In the meanwhile, they may drink or inject the bleach [just kidding] and read the Bible to achieve their hearts renewal. Hell is the most serious life's adverse event.

The Pfizer recently announced their covid-19 experimental vaccine List of the side effects and adverse events (total 1,291). The side effect #1 in this List is the 1p36 Deletion Syndrome. This side effect contributes to the current A.S.S. and S.S. plandemic. The symptoms of the 1p36 deletion syndrome include severe intellectual disability. Most affected individuals do not speak, or speak only a few words. They have temper tantrums, bite themselves, or exhibit other behavior problems.

Most of them get structural abnormalities of their brain, and seizures occur in more than half of individuals with this disorder. People with the 1p36 deletion syndrome have their vision and hearing problems, abnormalities of the skeleton, heart, gastrointestinal system, kidneys, or genitalia. The people with this syndrome can turn into zombie-like creatures.

Wikipedia - 1p36 Deletion Syndrome

Zombies. Photo by cottonbro studio (Image free to use)

Sounds like a disaster? The CDC campaign that used a reference to zombies to promote preparedness for different emergencies and disasters is now retired.

CHAPTER 2

WHAT IS THE HUMAN HEART?

No, this is not a textbook but we all need to know it. The human heart is a four-chambered muscular organ, serving as the primary pump and driving force within the circulatory system of the human body. The heart has a special form of muscle, called the cardiac muscle. It is able to beat on its own, without nervous system control. Extrinsic control of the heart rate and rhythm is achieved via autonomic nervous system impulses and specific hormones that alter the conductive and contractile properties of heart muscle. This information is just the basics that all should know.

A word "heart" has many synonyms and similar words: kindness, feelings, good-heartedness, empathy, feeling, pity, humanity, softheartedness, mercy, regard, bigheartedness, compassion, love, charity, largeheartedness, sensitivity, generosity, ruth, kindheartedness, commiseration, warmheartedness, benevolence, humanitarianism, benignity, sympathy, affection, kindliness, affinity, sensibility, responsiveness, philanthropy, benignancy, humanism, rapport, humaneness, goodwill, altruism.

It also has many antonyms: indifference, callousness, hard-heartedness, mercilessness, pitilessness, coldness, inhumanity, hatred, disinterest.

The heart is often used in spiritual writings. It is seen as the main source of what happens in our spiritual lives, which explains why love is associated with the heart - the real love comes from the "core" of our being. Jesus is often depicted holding out his heart to the people, inviting them to take it and let Jesus' heart rule over their heart.

Jesus said: "Take my yoke upon you and learn from me, for I am meek and humble of heart; and you will find rest for yourselves" (Matthew 11:29).

The WEF is creating the new SIFI reality, and they now could be looking forward to changing all the definitions, replacing all information that we know with something else.

Jesus with his humble heart is not their hero. They announced that God is dead and they are acquiring the God's divine powers of creation and destruction. They might want to be portrayed in the wonderful paintings but I do not think it would happen.

Gaudenzio Ferrari. Stories of life and passion of Christ, fresco, 1513 (image from Wikipedia)

CHAPTER 3

CARDIOLOGY, SELF-RECYCLING, AND SUSTAINABILITY

Years ago, the *Forbes* published an article: *"Why Do We Inhale Oxygen And Exhale Carbon Dioxide?"* It said: "... you inhale oxygen because you need oxygen for some biological processes.... . The waste products of this processes are Carbon Dioxide and Water... ."

Carbon dioxide (CO2, an odorless, colorless gas) is produced by a body when it uses food for energy. Our blood carries carbon dioxide to our lungs and we exhale it out. When wearing the face masks, we inhale CO2 back. Some people drink their own urine to stay healthy. Some

Photo by Nadia Russ. New York City, October 27, 2022

might thinks that inhaling Carbon Dioxide can improve their health as well(?). Self-recycling to save our planet is a sustainable thing.

But wait! Some "... biologists recently discovered how to reprogram the molecular processes of aging in yeast cells, we haven't yet cracked the mysteries behind aging in the human brain", Candice Wang wrote in 2020 in her article *"Inhaling pure oxygen could keep your brain younger for longer."* This article said that nearly 16 million people in the US struggle with cognitive impairment, a debilitating condition that eventually robs individuals of their independence by chipping away at their memory, motor functions, and ability to concentrate or learn. But neuroscientists in Israel are trying to turn back the biological clock with one simple ingredient - oxygen, she wrote. Shai Efrati, a physician and director of the Sagol Center for Hyperbaric Medicine and Research at the Yitzhak Shamir Medical Center in Israel, has developed a new type of hyperbaric oxygen therapy that increases blood flow in the brain to prevent declining cognitive function in the brains of healthy, older adults. Hyperbaric oxygen therapy involves breathing in pure, highly concentrated oxygen in a pressurized chamber for a long duration.

Many people might do not know but the longest living people in modern history live in Abkhazia, the former autonomous republic of the USSR, located near Georgia. On the daily basis, the elders there are very active, they run up and down the mountains, laughing and dancing like the younger people. This happens because the Abkhasians are inhaling fresh air, they eat vegetables and fruits from their own gardens. They eat meat and drink milk not from supermarkets, but they grow their own cows, goats, and chickens. They make their own cheese and vine. Everything is toxins free. If they feel ill, they drink the world famous mineral water Borjomi, getting it from the next door Georgia.

The Borjomi springs were discovered by the Imperial Russian military in the 1820s. Today, Borjomi is exported to over 40 countries. This volcanic origin mineral water improves gallbladder, kidney and liver function; it cleanses body, increases immunity, helps in the treatment of digestive system. It has a good effect on heart. The ions accelerate biological processes, in particular, metabolism. Strangely, when it reaches the US customers, one serving of Borjomi has 23% DV of Sodium, which is too much, like in a slice of a pizza.

Abkhasians probably never heard about the sustainability developments, which are the UN's (United Nations) and WEF's Klaus Schwab projects. Many regular people do not know anything about them. In a few words, sustainability is a way for people to use the resources without resources running out. It means doing development without damaging or affecting environment. It is like this: there is an apple on a tree. You will be able to eat your tasty apple, but it still will be on the tree untouched. If Chinese were able to produce the plastic rice, the apples also can be made from some fiber or soft and juicy form of resin.

Our Common Future (Report), World Commission on Environment and Development said: "Sustainable development is development that meets the needs of the present without compromising the ability of future generations to meet their own needs."

The Unisex restrooms in the all types of public places and restaurants are also part of this development. There were

Photo by Nadia Russ. Unisex restroom in NYC's restaurant,
September 2022

a lot of SIFI studies and developments behind these unisex restrooms. The developers think that the people should be unisex too.

The insulation of a jacket that I recently bought was made of Ecoplume, which is the recycled-polyester made from 100% recycled plastic bottles. As an average person I should say: "That's great! Recycling is saving our planet." However, the Consumer Reports article *"Plastic Products Contain Toxic Chemicals"* quickly puts everything in places. It said that the researchers behind the study analyzed 34 everyday products made of 8 types of plastic to see how common toxicity might be. Seventy-four percent of the products they tested were toxic in some way. Muncke said that we've surrounded ourselves with plastic. The stuff has been used to package foods for the last 40 years; it's everywhere. It's fair that the average citizen would say that if it wasn't safe, it wouldn't be on supermarket shelves. In practice, however, it's actually not really well understood and we are still using known hazardous chemicals to make plastic packaging that leach into food. Some of the best-known examples include BPA, found in plastic water bottles, plastic storage containers, thermal paper receipts, and the lining of food cans, and

Photo by Nadia Russ. Jacket with insulation made from 100% recycled plastic bottles, October 30, 2022, NYC

Photo by Nadia Russ. Dog carrying plastic bottle in NYC's store, October 19, 2022

phthalates, found in many products, often used to make PVC plastics more flexible. Studies in humans link BPA to metabolic disease, obesity, infertility, and disorders like ADHD.

Studies in animals have also linked BPA to prostate and

mammary cancer, as well as brain development problems. Phthalates are known to affect hormones, Vandenberg said, which means they can alter the development of reproductive organs and alter sperm count in males. You're not going to just drop dead [from hormonal activity in plastics], but it could contribute to diseases that may manifest over decades, or it could affect unborn embryos and fetuses. And there are many more chemicals that we know far less about, as this latest study showed.

Should I toss my new sustainable toxic jacket now or later?.. When wearing it I feel like I am inside of a toxic plastic bottle. If it would get wet under rain, its chemicals would penetrate into my body through my skin. It looks like sustainability sounds good only theoretically.

Dr. James Kneller, MD, also wrote in his article *"Plastic and Heart Disease"* that since the 1960s, industrial chemical bisphenol A (BPA) has been used in the production of polycarbonate plastics and epoxy resins. These plastics are often used to coat the inside of food and water storage containers and can contaminate the food or liquid inside. In 2012 an article in *Circulation* first reported a direct link between higher exposure to BPA and a greater risk of developing heart disease later in life. The study checked urine samples after a 10-year period and found that those who had developed heart disease had higher urine BPA concentrations - compared to those who did not develop heart disease - at the beginning of the study. This study was performed on healthy adults and debunked the idea that BPA was harmful only to fetuses. The findings also add more evidence that BPA is another heart disease risk factor and that there is no safe level of exposure. Currently on this planet, the heart diseases are the #1 cause of deaths.

CHAPTER 4

COMPLIANCE, BIOENGINEERING FOODS, INTERNET OF THINGS, AND THE 4TH INDUSTRIAL REVOLUTION

The NYC's Subway trains started placing some suggestive, strange ads with intention to make people feel guilty. The ads say: "Compliance (com-pli-ance). We follow the rules. You carry on disrupting things." This ad does not explain who are "we" and who are "you." It does not say what kind rules "we follow." It does not say what kind "things" "you carry on disrupting." This is kind of ghosty ad. Everybody can interpret it the way they want or can, however, everyone can get a feelings of guilt for disrupting some things. This is the cloudy ad for the cloudy brains to make them more dull.

Photo by Nadia Russ. NYC's Subway train ad, October 29, 2022.

Before, people were fighting with the GMO foods producers. Today, the bioengineered foods filled the stores shelves. How big is the difference? They are almost the same. Bioengineered foods are foods that have had a gene from different species of plant or other organism added to "improve" the existing characteristics. According to encyclopedia, the general purpose of bioengineering is to create plants that are in some way superior to the current plants being used. New BE products continue to be developed and not all are included in the existing already List. Those who are selling the bioengineered foods must make their disclosure. But do they?

Many scientists agreed that these scientific experiments are not safe. The widespread presence of bioengineered foods in the US's supermarkets is based on the premise that all these foods can be presumed safe unless proven otherwise. The aggressive money makers and the sales agents are refusing to recognize the risks of unpredictable negative side effects and it is just wrong and dangerous.

This is the current List of bioengineered foods: Alfalfa, Apple (Arctic varieties), Canola, Corn, Cotton, Eggplant (BARI Bt Begun varieties), Papaya (ringspot virus-resistant varieties), Pineapple (pink flesh varieties), Potato, Salmon (AquAdvantage), Soybean, Squash (summer), Sugarbeet.

Photo by Nadia Russ. NYC's Midtown, September 2022

Different people react to bioengineering developments differently. Some got involved immediately, shewing all those bioengineered foods with a smile on their faces. Others said "no way" using their own words.

The planet is now moving fast to the new SIFI dimension called *Internet of Things*. Klaus Schwab is everybody's "boss" now, no matter who yo,u are and what you do - in politics, in private sector, or even if you are a president of your country. Everyone "must" comply with what Schwab said. But many people still do not know who he is and never heard about his SIFI project. According to Schwab, everything and everyone should be connected to internet. At one of his WEF (World Economic Forum) SIFI meetings, he said that in 10 years we will have the implants in our brains and he will know immediately what each person in the audience feels.

Klaus Schwab talking about having brain implants that will allow him know immediately what the audience think.
https://www.youtube.com/watch?v=64dKPF866mM

Schwab is also famous for saying the while ago about "penetrating" the political cabinets globally. He

Klaus Schwab and WEF supporters Merkel, Xi, Clinton, Ivanka Trump, Kerry, Trump (?), Macron, other.

Klaus Schwab and WEF supporters Biden, Bush, Netanyahu, Putin, Trudeau, Zelenskyy, Gates, other.

mentioned such names as Merkel (Germany), Putin (Russia), Trudeau (Canada), Macron (France), Argentina's President... . He did a great job doing it. He probably has some charisma. It looks like no one can resist.

Photo by Nadia Russ, Flyers 'Unf*ck The World' and 'Anti-Bullsh*t', NYC, April 2021

However, recently, Alberta's new Premier Danielle Smith "fired off" on Klaus Schwab and his World Economic Forum. She said that it is offensive. She said that the people who should be directing government are the people who vote for them, and the people who vote for her and for her colleagues, or people who live in Alberta and who are affected by the government decisions. Danielle Smith said that until that organization [WEF] stops bragging about how much control they have over political leaders, she has no interest in being involved with them; her focus is there in Alberta, solving problems for Albertans with the mandate from Albertans.

It sounds like the new Alberta's Premier wants Schwab to be more discreet about his penetration of the political cabinets before she would start collaborating with him.

Many people admire Elon Musk for his "intelligence" and his support of free speech that contradicts the globalists' NWO agenda. However, he was spotted at the MET's Gala in NYC wearing his white New World Order jacket in Latin *"Novus Ordo Seclorum."* The photographers barely could capture the white on white sign, it was almost invisible on pictures. It is obvious that Musk did not want to be widely publicized as the NWO and the Great Reset supporter, promoter and active participant. He is also the Klaus Schwab WEF's Young Global Leader, class 2008. His Neuralink company is working now on the brain implants project, the chips for the human brains, which are the Klaus Schwab's dream. The logo of Elon Musk's Tesla, where he is co-founder and CEO, strangely reminds the Baphomet's head. However, Musk said it was just the stylized "T".

The *"Novus Ordo Seclorum"* means the "New order of the ages." It is the second of two mottos added on the

Investment Watch

A fine selection of independent media sources

IWB | Newsletters/RSS | About | Economic Calendar

Elon Musk Wears "New World Order" Jacket to the Met Gala, Bloomberg Confirms Elon Is a Young Global Leader for Klaus Schwab/WEF/Great Reset

April 16, 2022 5:17 pm by IWB

Share

imgur

Elon Musk wearing *Novus Ordo Seclorum* (NOW) jacket at the Met's Gala in NYC

https://www.investmentwatchblog.com/elon-musk-wears-new-world-order-jacket-to-the-met-gala-bloomberg-confirms-elon-is-a-young-global-leader-for-klaus-schwab-wef-great-reset

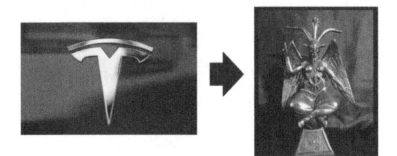

Tesla's logo looks like head of Baphomet (sculpture by unknown artist)

Reverse of the Great Seal of the United States

reverse of the Great Seal of the United States (the first motto is *Annuit cœptis*).

So what is wrong with this *Novus Ordo Seclorum*? This new order means the total control of the Earth population. It means the regular folks will have no opportunity to exercise their free speech, act the way they want, and even think freely. It is called the dictature of the ruling class or a few ruling people. In this case, it looks like the dictature of WEF, Satan that they worship, and the Artificial Intelligence. The free will no more. This is very selfish. No wonder that many people do not like Klaus Schwab and what he is doing. These people are constantly banned from the internet websites for saying what they think. This is why they put their thoughts on the sheets of paper and glue them to the electrical utility pole, building walls or other surfaces on the streets like in old good times. Those flyers would be also removed but not that fast.

Our planet now is rotating around Klaus Schwab and his World Economic Forum. His Great Reset project launched in 2020. He is now 84, and kicking.

Schwab in 2011 (photo from Wikipedia)

Klaus M. Schwab born on March 30, 1938. He is a German engineer, economist and founder of the WEF. He has acted as the WEF's chairman since founding the organization in 1971. He wrote several books and one of them is *"The Fourth Industrial Revolution."* The subject of this book explores the ideas he has popularized - "the internet of things".

The political scientist Klaus-Gerd Giesen argued that the dominant ideology of the 4th Industrial Revolution is transhumanism. Steven Poole reviewed Schwab's book in The Guardian (January 2017). In his article *"The Fourth Industrial Revolution review - adapt to new technology or perish"* he wrote: "Schwab shows in an appendix that he does know that the idea that 'digital technology knows no borders' is simply false, and throughout he is careful to

41

be even-handed about the upsides and downsides of every technology he discusses. Artificial intelligence might be super-useful, or it might constitute an existential threat to humanity." Biotechnology might cure all diseases, or it might create a schism of bio-inequality. The overall problem is that this is basically all Schwab does: describing some future development or its opposite and essentially asking: "Is this brilliant? Or is this terrible?" The purchaser of such a book might expect the author to have a reasoned opinion on the matter. Instead, Schwab offers policy recommendations, which - perhaps by design - are vague enough to be useful to a politician of any stripe. Indeed, the book climaxes with a rather lovely plea for everyone to work together in a "new cultural renaissance" that apparently will depend on some kind of cosmic spirituality. The fourth industrial revolution might lead to a dehumanising dystopia, Schwab allows soberly. On the other hand, we could use it "to lift humanity into a new collective and moral consciousness based on a shared sense of destiny."

Here is the List of the WEF's Young Global Leaders who graduated in 1993-2021: https://plebeianresistance.substack.com/p/all-the-young-global-leaders-from?sr/. All the WEF's Young Global Leaders are obsessed with the Schwab's SIFI idea of *Internet of Things*, The Forth Industrial Revolution, and The Great Reset. His wish became very close to reality and he is thrilled.

Ivanka Trump is one of the Young Global Leaders as well, class 2015. Later, she was the President Trump's Advisor. The WH website archives proudly said: "...Ivanka has been included in Fortune magazine's prestigious "40

Under 40" list (2014) and was honored as a Young Global Leader by the World Economic Forum (2015)... ."

WEF, The Annual Meeting 2020, Ivanka Trump's Report.
https://www.youtube.com/watch?v=mIpMomsOWxA

Her father, the former President Donald Trump, who supposed to be the last hope of America, started the covid lockdowns and vaccination. He also told at the Coronavirus Task Force on April 23, 2020 briefing that injecting or drinking bleach may help to kill the virus.

The IndiaTV News wrote: "The American Association of Poison Control Center (AAPCC) has released the latest figures that show a substantial spike in deaths in the country due to accidental poisoning caused by the intake of bleach, household cleaners and other disinfectants over the past two months. This spike has been followed by

US's President Donald Trump's comments suggesting Americans could inject disinfectants to cure themselves of Coronavirus. ...   As per the official figures, the deaths due to household   disinfectants in the months January and February 2020 increased by 5% and 17% respectively while the months of March and April have seen an astronomical rise of 93% and 121%."

The WEF's training programs have been working for decades. It resulted in rapid advancement, placement and distribution through the world of many thousands of WEF-trained operatives. Here is the recent list of the Young Global Leaders (109), class 2022:

1. Joud Abdel Majeid, Deputy Chief Financial Officer, BlackRock, USA.

2. Matthew Katz, Global Head of Data Science, Blackstone Group, USA.

3. Usman Ahmed, Head of Global Public Policy and Research, Paypal, Inc., USA.

4. Kaitlyn Sadtler, Investigator; Chief of Section, Immunoengineering, National Institutes of Health, USA.

5. Colin Allred, Congressman from Texas (D), 32nd District, U.S. House of Representatives, USA.

6. Alaa Murabit, Director, Health (PAC), UN High-Level Commissioner and SDG Advocate, Bill & Melinda Gates Foundation, USA.

7. Jessica Beckerman, Co-Founder and Chief Medical Officer, Muso, USA.

8. Eugene Chung, Chief Executive Officer and Founder, Penrose Studios, USA.

9. Joy Buolamwini, Founder and Executive Director, Algorithmic Justice League, USA.

10. Eugene Chung, Chief Executive Officer and Founder, Penrose Studios, USA.

11. Matt Dalio, Founder and Chair, Endless OS, USA.

12. Vilas Dhar, President and Trustee, Patrick J. McGovern Foundation, USA.

13. Margot Edelman, General Manager, Edelman, USA.

14. Badruun Gardi, LOEB Fellow, Harvard University Graduate School of Design, USA.

15. Bicheng Han, Founder and Chief Executive Officer, BrainCo, USA.

16. Jennifer (Jen) Auerbach-Rodriguez, Managing Director - MLWM Strategic Growth Markets, Merrill Lynch, USA.

17. Orenzo "Perry" Hollowell, Head, Equities and Sustainable Investing, CFI Partners, USA.

18. John R. Tyson, Chief Financial Officer, Tyson Foods, USA.

19. Kiah Williams, Co-Founder and Managing Director, Supporting Initiatives to Redistribute Unused Medicine - SIRUM, USA.

20. Mark Stoffels, Senior Vice-President, Connected Care

North America, Philips, USA.

21. Enass Abo-Hamed, Chief Executive Officer, H2GO Power Ltd., United Kingdom.

22. Sahar Albazar, Parliament Member & Deputy Chair of Foreign Affairs Committee, Egyptian Parliament, Egypt.

23. Mohammed Alghanim, Group Chief Executive Officer, Hamad S. Al-Ghanim Group, Kuwait.

24. Safiya Al-Jabry, Executive Director, Small and Micro Enterprise Promotion Service (SMEPS), Yemen.

25. Hamad AlMahmeed, Director General, Prime Minister's Office, Bahrain.

26. Abdulrahman Essa Al-Mannai, Chief Executive Officer, Milaha Group, Qatar.

27. Mark Boris Andrijanič, Member of the Governing Board, European Institute of Innovation and Technology, United Kingdom.

28. Jaideep Bansal, Chief Executive Officer, Global Himalayan Expedition (GHE), India.

29. Bolor-Erdene Battsenge, State Secretary, Ministry of Digital Development, Mongolia.

30. Venetia Bell, Group Chief Sustainability Officer; Head, Strategy, Gulf International Bank (GIB), United Kingdom.

31. Natalie Black, Her Majesty's Trade Commissioner for Asia Pacific, Department for International Trade, Singapore.

32. Noor Boodai, Chief Executive Officer, TenX, Kuwait.

33. Fares Bugshan, Chief Executive Officer, Bugshan Investment, Saudi Arabia.

34. Yanqing (Kenny) Cai, Co-Founder and Chief Executive Officer, BottleDream, People's Republic of China.

35. Freddy Castro, Chief Executive Officer, Banca de las Oportunidades, Colombia.

36. Raghav Chadha, Member of Parliament - Upper House (Rajya Sabha), Government of the National Capital Territory of Delhi, India.

37. Claire Cormier Thielke, Country Head, Greater China, Hines Asia Pacific, Hong Kong SAR, China.

38. Bárbara Luiza Coutinho do Nascimento, State Prosecutor, Rio de Janeiro State Prosecutor's Office, Brazil.

39. Maria Eugenia del Castillo Cabrera, Envoy of the Vice-President of the Dominican Republic, The Presidency of the Dominican Republic, Dominican Republic.

40. Clarissa Delgado, Co-Founder and Chief Executive Officer, Teach For the Philippines, Philippines.

41. Soraya Djermoun, Geopolitical expert, author and Entrepreneur, Kheyma, Algeria.

42. Ola Doudin, Co-Founder and Chief Executive Officer, BitOasis, United Arab Emirates.

43. Esra Eczacıbaşı Coşkun, Member of the Board of Directors and Group Digital Transformation Coordinator, Eczacıbaşı Holding, Türkiye.

44. Ilwad Elman, Chief Operating Officer, Elman Peace Centre, Canada.

45. Amal Enan, Chief Investment Officer, American University in Cairo, Egypt.

46. Mykhailo Fedorov, Vice-Prime Minister, Minister of Digital Transformation, Ministry of Digital ransformation of Ukraine, Ukraine.

47. Daniel Feldman, Founder & Architect, Zona Industrial Taller de Arquitectura, Colombia.

48. Sean Fraser, Minister of Immigration, Refugees and Citizenship, Citizenship and Immigration Canada, Canada.

49. Luana Génot, Executive Director, Brazilian Identities Institute, Brazil.

50. Gaurav Gupta, Founder and Chief Executive Officer, Gabit, India.

51. Radhika Gupta, Managing Director and Chief Executive Officer, Edelweiss Mutual Fund, India.

52. Kim Hallwood, Head, Corporate Sustainability, HSBC Bank Canada, Canada.

53. Sophia Hamblin Wang, Chief Operating Officer, Mineral Carbonation International (MCi), Australia.

54. Miku Hirano, Chief Executive Officer, Cinnamon, Japan.

55. Frederic Hoffmann, Member of the Board, MAVA Foundation, Switzerland.

56. Caroline Blanch Israel, Managing Director and Partner, Boston Consulting Group, Australia.

57. Mmaki Jantjies, Head of Innovation, Telkom, South Africa.

58. Manasi Joshi, Athlete, Sports Authority of India, India.

59. Wissam Joubran, Composer, Performer, Luthier, Le Trio Joubran, Palestinian Territories.

60. Freshta Karim, Founding Director, Charmaghz Cultural and Services Organization, United Kingdom.

61. Christer Kjos, Chief Executive Officer, Canica Holding, Switzerland.

62. Danae Kyriakopoulou, Distinguished Policy Fellow, Grantham Research Institute, London School of Economics and Political Science, United Kingdom.

63. Irina Lachowski, Chief Executive Officer, RenovaBR, Brazil.

64. Yashovardhan Lohia, Executive Director and Chief Sustainability Officer, Indorama Ventures, Thailand.

65. Siwan (Swan) Lu, Principal, Zurich Global Ventures, Switzerland.

66. Zoya Lytvyn, Head, Osvitoria, Ukraine.

67. Anne-Laure Malauzat, Partner; Lead, Social Impact Practice, Europe, Middle East and Africa; Chief Diversity, Equity and Inclusion Officer, Middle East, Bain & Company, United Arab Emirates.

68. Ritesh Malik, Founder, Innov8 Coworking, India.

69. Esha Mansingh, Executive Vice-President, Corporate Affairs and Investor. Relations, Imperial Logistics, South Africa.

70. Eva Maydell, Member of the European Parliament, European Parliament, Belgium.

71. Philip Meissner, Founder and Director, European Center for Digital Competitiveness, Germany.

72. James Kwame Mensah, Senior Lecturer, University of Ghana, Ghana.

73. James Mnyupe, Presidential Economic Adviser; Green Hydrogen Commissioner, Office of the President of Namibia, Namibia.

74. Inna Modja, Land Ambassador, United Nations Convention to Combat Desertification (UNCCD), Portugal.

75. Nasreen Ali Mohamed, Founder and Chief Executive Officer, Afrikapu Ltd, Kenya.

76. Françoise Moudouthe, Chief Executive Officer, African Women's Development Fund, Ghana.

77. Tom Mustill, Director, Gripping Films Ltd, United Kingdom.

78. Zuriel Naiker, Managing Director: Industry (Middle East & Africa), and Sales (Africa), Marsh & McLennan Companies, South Africa.

79. Lesley Ndlovu, Chief Executive Officer, African Risk Capacity (ARC), South Africa.

80. Billy Wai-Lung Ng, Assistant Professor, School of

Pharmacy, The Chinese University of Hong Kong, Hong Kong SAR, China.

81. Yoichi Ochiai, Associate Professor, University of Tsukuba, Japan.

82. Eva Otieno, Africa Strategist, Standard Chartered Bank Kenya Ltd, Kenya.

83. Ioana Patriniche, Managing Director / Head of Investor Relations, Deutsche Bank, United Kingdom.

84. Mia Perdomo, Co-Founder and Chief Executive Officer, Aequales, Colombia.

85. Carlo Perez-Arizti, Partner, Baker McKenzie, Mexico.

86. Sarah Rawson, Regional Head of Business Management EMEA, Swiss Re Services Limited, United Kingdom.

87. Juan Carlos Rincón, Editor of the Opinion Section, El Espectador, Colombia.

88. Sara Saeed Khurram, Chief Executive Officer and Co-Founder, Sehat Kahani, Pakistan.

89. Suhail Sameer, Chief Executive Officer, Resilient Innovation Private Limited (BharatPe), India.

90. Zou Shasha, Founder and Chief Executive Officer, AHA Entertainment, People's Republic of China.

91. Shen Peng, Founder and Chief Executive Officer, Shuidi Company, People's Republic of China

92. Yichen Shen, Founder and Chief Executive Officer, Lightelligence, People's Republic of China.

93. Naif Sheshah, Assistant Deputy Governor for Planning and Development & Chief Digital Officer, Communications and Information Technology Commission (CITC), Saudi Arabia.

94. Mayank Singhal, Global Head of Private Equity and Venture Capital, Abu Dhabi Growth Fund (ADG), United Arab Emirates.

95. Omar Sultan Al Olama, Minister of State for Artificial Intelligence, Digital Economy and Remote Work Applications, Office of the Prime Minister of the United Arab Emirates, United Arab Emirates.

96. Christy Lei Sun, Chief Marketing Officer, Yatsen Global, People's Republic of China.

97. Steve Suryadinata, Managing Director, BSA Land, Indonesia.

98. Saad Hayat Tamman, Member – Strategic Reforms and Implementation Unit, Office of the Prime Minister of Pakistan, Pakistan.

99. Anderson Tanoto, Managing Director, RGE, Singapore.

100. Sumayya Vally, Founder and Principal, Counterspace, South Africa.

101. Dominic Wadongo, Group Head of Operational Risk, Equity Group Holdings Plc, Kenya.

102. Sun Xuemei, Chairperson, Beijing All in One Public Welfare Foundation, People's Republic of China.

103. Yuito Yamada, Partner, McKinsey & Company, Japan.

104. Luhui Yan, Founder and Chief Executive Officer, Carbonstop, People's Republic of China.

105. Yeoh Keong Hann, Executive Director, YTL Power Generation, Malaysia.

106. Yousef Yousef, Chief Executive Officer, LG Sonic B.V., Netherlands.

107. Boju Zhang, Secretary General, Ginkgo Foundation, People's Republic of China.

108. Daniel Zhang Xianming, Vice President, Broad Group, People's Republic of China.

109. Jinxing Zheng, Division Head, Professor, Institute of Plasma Physics, Chinese Academy of Sciences, People's Republic of China.

WEF quietly launched the Forth Industrial Revolution (4IR) for the Earth Initiative in 2017. It is a collaboration among WEF, Stanford University and PwC. It is funded through the Mava Foundation. In 2018, WEF quietly launched another project, called the Earth BioGenome. The aim of this project is to sequence the genomes of every organism on Earth, all eukaryotic species. For five years the MSM was quiet about these project or dropped only a few sentences.

The Wikipedia has such page "Earth BioGenome Project." It said that it is "an initiative that aims to *sequence and catalog the genomes of all of Earth's currently described eukaryotic species over a period of ten years.* The initiative would produce an open DNA database of biological information that provides a platform for scientific research and supports environmental and conservation initiatives. A scientific paper presenting the vision for the project was published in *PNAS* in April 2018, and the project officially launched November 1, 2018."

The Eukaryotic species are organisms, composed of one or more cells containing visibly evident nuclei and organelles. The eukaryotic species include humans, animals, plants, fungi, and protozoa.

In the US, the staff at Naval Health Research Center (NHRC) added whole genome sequencing capability to their surveillance program. NHRC brought on scientists and lab technicians to support this work and bioinformatics, which increased their database and

Also in 2017, WEF launched the Fourth Industrial Revolution (4IR) for the Earth Initiative, a collaboration among WEF, Stanford University and PwC, and funded through the Mava Foundation.[99] In 2018, WEF announced that one project within this initiative was to be the Earth BioGenome Project, the aim of which is to sequence the genomes of every organism on Earth.[100]

The World Economic Forum is working to eliminate plastic pollution, stating that by 2050 it will consume 15% of the global carbon budget and will pass by its weight fishes in the world's oceans. One of the methods is to achieve circular economy.[101][102]

The theme of the 2020 World Economic Forum annual meeting was 'Stakeholders for a Cohesive and Sustainable World'. Climate change and sustainability were central themes of discussion. Many argued that GDP is failed to represent correctly the wellbeing and that fossil fuel subsidies should be stopped. Many of the participants said that a better capitalism is needed. Al Gore summarized the ideas in the conference as: "The version of capitalism we have today in our world must be reformed".[103]

The 4ᵗʰ Industrial Revolution launched by WEF in 2017
Wikipedia's screenshot, November 26, 2022

Earth BioGenome Project

Article   Talk

The **Earth BioGenome Project (EBP)** is an initiative that aims to sequence and catalog the genomes of all of Earth's currently described eukaryotic species over a period of ten years.[1] The initiative would produce an open DNA database of biological information that provides a platform for scientific research and supports environmental and conservation initiatives.[2] A scientific paper presenting the vision for the project was published in *PNAS* in April 2018,[3] and the project officially launched November 1, 2018.[4]

Earth BioGenome Project

Duration	November 1, 2018 – 2028
Website	www.earthbiogenome.org ↗

Page Earth BioGenome Project

Wikipedia's screenshot, November 26, 2022

analysis capabilities. Lab technicians worked to test samples, identify candidates for WGS, and ultimately perform the sequencing reactions.

People from the US, who all their lives lived enjoying the free speech, liberties and freedoms, have to learn a lot from the WEF before they will be able to move in to the digitized cultural Marxist SIFI reality of the Internet of Things. Would they even agree to do this?? Some agreed without asking any questions.

The Young Global Leader Usman Ahmed is the Head of Global Public Policy and Research at PayPal, Inc., USA. He graduated the WEF's program in 2022, and BOOM!!!... In October of 2022, PayPal has announced their new policy update that was coming to action in November 2022. This update said that PayPal would charge $2,500 fine every time its members would exercise the free speech. They called it the violation and the misinformation. The company stated that determinations of which messages violated the policy would be made at "PayPal's sole discretion." The PayPal becoming the accuser, the prosecutor, the judge, and the fines collector. I recognize in it the communist's totalitarian power in action. I was born in a communist country and I truly do not like it, no matter from who this "innovation" coming, from WEF, Biden, Trump, or Devil himself. For sure it is not coming from God. We are witnessing now many significant changes in this, one time free society.

When I started writing this chapter, I read the news: "The NY Supreme Court ruled to reinstate, with back pay, workers who were fired for refusing vaccines." It means that the people, who were struck by A.S.S. (Amazing Stupidity Syndrome), were wrong and eventually their decisions were reversed. The Washington Times wrote: ""... The court cited evidence that the shots do not thwart transmission within the workplace. Being vaccinated does not prevent an individual from contracting or transmitting COVID-19," the Monday [October 24, 2022] decision by Judge Ralph J. Porzio said. New York City fired around 1,400 workers, including many cops and firefighters, for being unvaccinated after former Mayor Bill de Blasio instituted a mandate for city workers, according to the Fox News. Judge Porzio said former Health Commissioner David Chokshi overstepped his authority with "arbitrary and capricious" orders that effectively said who could report to work and who cannot. Mayor Eric Adams, a Democrat, has dropped many COVID-19 rules but stood by the mandate on city workers... . The court said the employees could return to work on Oct. 25, 2022."

This is just a small victory of the common sense. To finish with the all huge mess, a lot of fixing and many hearts renewals needed. And it can be done only by the people who do not suffer from A.S.S. or S.S..

CHAPTER 5

FREE RADICALS ARE
IN
THE AIR

Years ago, someone told me that life is a dangerous thing. I did not think that way then. But now, I agree with this saying. Recently, I received a promotional email in my mail box offering to order the new kratom products that were free with free shipping. I was associating kratom with marijuana because I saw recently many stores in NYC with this name and all of them had the marijuana leaf logo on signage. I do not like this kind stuff and I would not try it even if someone would beg me to try. However, I am sure many people would order it. After receiving this email I checked what kratom was. It was not Marijuana but Mitragyna speciosa.

**Happy Hippo company sends away free samples of kratom
(happyhippo.com)**

According to webmd.com, kratom is a tree native to Southeast Asia. The leaves contain a chemical called mitragynine, which works like opioids, such as morphine. Using kratom can be unsafe. It is banned in some states and countries due to serious safety concerns. The US FDA has warned consumers to avoid using products containing kratom. Rare but serious effects have been reported in people who use it, including psychiatric, cardiovascular, gastrointestinal and respiratory problems. A small number of deaths have been linked to kratom products. Kratom is addictive.

Kratom - Mitragyna speciosa. Photo by Uomo vitruviano
(photo from Wikipedia)

Another SIFI-linked product is marijuana. It can be purchased in NYC 24/7 everywhere, from the small mobile

Photo by Nadia Russ. Kratom store at 1420 Broadway, New York, January 21, 2023

stores or from   the large trucks, that appeared all over. This product helps to adopt to the new cosmic reality.

Photo by Nadia Russ. Marijuana for sell in NYC, August 2022

In the most prestigious areas, such as near **MOMA** (Museum of Modern Art) in Midtown of Manhattan, at 53rd Street, the truck sells the organic marijuana. In NYC, there are the marijuana products for all types of people and for the all walks of life.

The covid PCR and rapid testing booths have appeared on every corner as well. They are also signifying the new times, helping people to get feeling of being connected to each other and another reality. In some way these covid testing booths are like the Mark Zuckerberg's Metaverse. Mark Zuckerberg is also the WEF's Young Global Leader, class 2004.

The metaverse is a hypothetical iteration of the Internet as a single, universal and immersive virtual world that is facilitated by the use of virtual reality and augmented

Photo by Nadia Russ. Truck sales organic marijuana near MOMA, at the West 53rd Street, NY NY, August 2022

reality headsets. In colloquial use, a metaverse is a network of 3D virtual worlds focused on social connection. However, many people these days not need those headsets to live in 3D virtual worlds, they are already in another dimention.

Klaus Schwab says that his organization is attempting to fundamentally change human beings, and that his industrial revolution will not change what you are doing. It changes you. Yuval Noah Harari explained what Klaus Schwab means. Harari said in his video that it's you who are changed. In the past, many tyrants and governments wanted to [hack millions of people], but nobody understood biology well enough, and nobody had

Photo by Nadia Russ. Covid testing booth on 23ʳᵈ Street of Manhattan, NYC, November 2022

Yuval Noah Harari supports and promotes the WEF agenda. He is talking about hacking human beings
https://www.youtube.com/watch?v=8qhZXyZ_kpl

enough computing power and data to hack millions of people. Neither the Gestapo nor the KGB could do it. But soon, at least some corporations and governments will be able to systematically hack all the people. He added: "We are now hackable animals."

He also said that this merging of human life with technology will not benefit the average man or woman so that he or she may improve his or her own future, but that a handful of "elites" will not only "build digital dictatorships" for themselves but "gain the power to re-engineer the future of life itself. Because once you can hack something, you can usually also engineer it."

According to Harari's book *"Sapiens,"* progress is an illusion; the Agricultural Revolution was "history's biggest fraud," and liberal humanism is a religion no more founded on reality than any other. Harari writes: "The Sapiens regime on earth has so far produced little that we can be proud of." I agree with this Harari's saying, based on what is going on now.

Harari wrote in his book *"Sapiens"*: "In itself, the universe is only a meaningless hodge-podge of atoms. Nothing is beautiful, sacred, or sexy – but human feelings make it so. ... Take away human feelings, and you are left with a bunch of molecules." He also wrote: "Any meaning that people ascribe to their lives is just a delusion. ... Life has no meaning, and people don't need to create any meaning. They just need to realize that there is no meaning, and thus be liberated from the suffering caused by our attachments and our identification with empty phenomena."

Harari said the human life has no meaning. However, his life has meaning. He dedicated it promoting WEF and its agenda. The Klaus Schwab's life also has meaning, he wants complete the 4th Industrial Revolution and his Great Reset, turning the humans into transhumans, connected to internet. The Young Global Leaders also have meaningful lives, they are helping Klaus Schwab to make SIFI the reality as soon as possible. The scientists want discover something they do not know yet, the business people want get as rich as possible, the writers dedicate their lives to write a bestseller, the artists want create the unique paintings, the actors want to get famous, the athletes want to win in competitions, the average folks dedicate their lives to creation of their families and growing children, the thieves want to steel as much as possible. Everyone's life has meaning.

Yuval Noah Harari wants to see humans liberated from the suffering causes, from attachments, feelings and identification. It looks like he was suffering a lot from rejection(s) or misunderstanding. It looks like he was burned out. We all did more or less. But this is not a reason to punish the whole planet, turning its people into a bunch of molecules with no feelings and attachments. Suffering can changes people, making them more kind or cruel. But still a few burned out people should not be punishing the whole planet, turning its people into the red-blooded robots, manipulated remotely.

If this 4th Industrial Revolution with The Great Reset would happen and people would turn into the digital devices-type creatures, controlled by the Artificial Intelligence, this world would become a very boring place. The feelings make our lives and this world fascinating. Such strong feeling as love, for example, inspires the composers to compose amazing music, the poets to create wonderful poetry, the artists to paint the great paintings. Even hate can inspire amazing creativity. There is no perfection without feelings and emotions because they bring the average creators onto another level, unreachable to people who have no feelings.

Normally, the humans born with feelings of beauty, internal and external. The little babies afraid of the ugly creatures. However, they get happy when they see the sun. flowers or their smiling mothers. Some adults lost their senses and feelings. They see no difference between the ugliness, internal or external, and beauty. They do not feel disgust smelling excrement, they see no difference if it is a flower or dodo. They are done with this life, they are just a bunch of molecules. But others still want to enjoy the beauty and perfection of this world, their feelings, emotions and attachments that make them happy, while the WEF wants cancel this enjoyment. It looks like the SIFI reality developers need no great music, no wonderful pieces of art, nor smell of roses. Or they are so obsessed with their project and so in a hurry, that they do not have time to think about any consequences of what they are doing.

A few months ago, I noticed that at the crossroads in Manhattan and Brooklyn of New York City the flyers "Messiah Is Here" appeared with a picture of a man wearing the black hat. They were glued to the back of the pedestrians signals boxes and other surfaces located so high that no human could reach them. Somebody did a huge work, running around the city with a ladder, or may be it was the aliens job. For many years so many people were waiting for Jesus to come, but it appeared that he did not come but the Messiah in a black hat is here instead... .

On November 6, 2022, at the Marathon day, I noticed that many of those flyers were partly removed or scratched out. All these flyers had text: "Long Live the Lubavitcher Rebbe King Messiah Forever." When I read "Lubavitcher," Russia came on my mind because I heard this name before in relation to Russia. I spent a few minutes online, and found a lot of interesting information. A man on the NYC's crossroads flyers was Menachem Mendel Schneerson (1902-1994), known to many as the Lubavitcher Rebbe. He was a Russian-born American Orthodox rabbi and the most recent Rebbe of the

Photo by Nadia Russ, Flyer "Messiah Is Here" was partly taken off, NYC's Upper East Side, November 6, 2022

Photo by Nadia Russ, Flyers "Messiah Is Here" were partly removed, NYC'; Upper East Side, November 6, 2022

Lubavitch Hasidic dynasty. The leader of Chabad-Lubavitch movement, he is considered one of the most influential Jewish leaders of the 20th century.

On November 16, I was at the Crown Heights in Brooklyn. There, I noticed that the next to the scratched off old flyers the new "Messiah Is Here" flyers were placed, but much higher.

While Lubavitcher Rebbe considered one of the most influential Jewish leader of 20th century, Vladimir Putin is not less influential Jewish leader of the 21st century. According to his Passport application his mother was a Jewish woman. An application for issuing a new

Photo by Nadia Russ, new flyers "Messiah Is Here" were placed

on Brooklyn's crossroads, November 16, 2022

Bladimir Putin's passport application saying that his mother was a Jewish woman Shelomova Maria Ivanovna.

passport of Russian citizen Putin Vladimir Vladimirovich of December 30, 2000, indicates that his father was Putin Vladimir Spiridonovich - Russian (marked on the right), and his mother was Shelomova Maria Ivanovna - Jewish (marked on the left).

In 2016, Putin has invited Jews to emigrate to Russia because there was increase of anti-Semitic violence in Europe. He said that Jews should return to Russia: "Let them [Jews] come to us then. ... During the Soviet period they were leaving the country, and now they should return."

The theyeshivaworld.com wrote in 2020 that Jewish communities in Russia have seen an unprecedented renaissance of Jewish religious life under Putin, including the return of dozens of shuls and buildings that were confiscated from Jewish communities in the past, establishment of the $50 million Jewish Museum and Tolerance Center in Moscow with encouragement of Putin, and more recently, the building of a Jewish youth center in the Far Eastern Russian city of Birobidzhan.

The "Putin's rabbi", Berel Lazar (Shlomo Dov Pinchas Lazar) born May 19, 1964 in Italy. His parents were among the first emissaries of Rabbi Menachem Mendel Schneerson. Now, Berel Lazar is an Orthodox Chabad-Lubavitch Hasidic rabbi. He began his service in Russia in 1990. Known for his close friendship with Putin, since 2000, he has been a Chief Rabbi of Russia and chairman of the Federation of Jewish Communities of Russia and Federation of Jewish Communities of the CIS. In September 2005, Lazar became a member of the Public Chamber of Russia.

Vladimir Putin with Berel Lazar during the World Holocaust Forum in Jerusalem, January 23, 2020. Photo credit: www.jpost.com, Sputnik, Alexei Nikolsky/Kremlin

After beginning of the current Russia - Ukraine conflict, when the international community started boycotting Russia everywhere, seventy-five leading Russian rabbis have reiterated their collective commitment to "not abandoning their communities and staying with them [in Russia] to provide spiritual, psychological and emotional support, no matter how complicated things get," according to the Federation of Jewish Communities of Russia the statement issued in an emergency conference in Moscow. The rabbis, led by Chief Rabbi Berel Lazar, said in the statement, "Our role is not to involve ourselves in domestic or geopolitics. We are shocked that some individuals not only believe that rabbis have a duty to jeopardize their communities by engaging in political activities or even to abandon their community altogether as a form of political protest. ... The word "Ukraine" was not mentioned in the statement, the Jerusalem Post said. The Russian rabbis refused to leave Russia.

As someone who was born in Ukraine when it was still part of the USSR, I would never believe that Russians and Ukrainians would be killing each other one day. It is still difficult to believe it. Both of my parents were Russians, who came to Ukraine in their 30s, then I was born. They died in Ukraine from the natural causes before this nationalistic craziness started. I am glad they did not see it.

A few months ago, I read in Yahoo! News an article by Ben

Adler *"Ukrainian mayor, heralded by many, is ultranationalist."* It was an article about Konotop, a small city where I was born and spent first 15 years of my life. When I was there, everything was different, quiet and peaceful. There were no anti-Russians or anti-Jews tendencies in the authorities politics. However, like everywhere, some regular Ukrainians might did not like the Russian or Jewish people. But it was seldom seeing or heard. The Yahoo*!* article wrote on March 2022 that Artem Semenikhin, the mayor of the small city of Konotop, in northeastern Ukraine, stood on a planter outside the City Council and announced to a crowd that Russian soldiers had told him they would raze the city to the ground with their artillery if it did not surrender. Then Semenikhin asked the crowd whether they wanted to fight anyway, and the response was overwhelmingly in favor.... . In 2015, shortly after Semenikhin took office, the Jerusalem Post reported that he "refused to fly the city's official flag at the opening meeting of the city council because he objected to the star of David emblazoned on it." Alan MacLeod, a writer for the far-left website MintPress News, noted on Twitter that in Semenikhin's interview with PBS, conducted remotely via video, one could see a painting of Ukrainian nationalist icon Stepan Bandera in the background. During the early part of World War II, Bandera led a faction of Organization of Ukrainian nationalists, an openly anti-Semitic organization that collaborated with Nazi Germany and killed Polish and Jewish civilians. At the time, Nazi troops were invading the Soviet Union, which Ukrainian nationalists were hoping to break away from.... .

There could be many explanations of this nonsense war, which actually started many years ago, when the old government was overthrown and the new Ukrainian government restricted its people from speaking Russian, prioritizing everything Ukrainian. They said that Ukraine is for Ukrainians only, while there were many Russians and other nationalities people who born and lived there all their life and who were the Russian-speaking people. They felt stripped out of everything. After Putin started in 2022 the "denazification operation," Zelenskyy, the President of Ukraine, told the Russian speakers in Donbass that if they love Russia, they need to go and to look for a place in Russia. For more than decade the Ukrainian nationalists do not tolerate there anything from abroad. It looks like they want to be a clean, pure blood nation, just like in the Nazi Germany, where the laws were introduced to ensure blood purity. In Nazi Germany, anyone who acted outside of these laws was deemed to have committed the crime of "rassenschande," which translates roughly as "racial pollution" or "racial" crime.

In February of 2022, the Ukrainian MP Kira Rudik said on Fox News that she is fighting for the New World Order (aka The Global Reset): "It's not only fight for Ukraine but for this New World Order for the democratic countries."

It appears that the Ukrainian nationalists are slightly behind the time. The people they admire have no problems with the interracial marriages. Daughter of Bill Gates, Jennifer Gates married Egyptian Nayel Nassar in a Muslim ceremony. Mark Zuckerberg married American-Chinese Priscilla Chan. Prince Harry married a black woman Meghan Markle. John Legend married a Caucasian Chrissy Teigen. There are many interracial couples there.

If Ukrainians were fighting for the New World Order, they should know by now what it means. They should know that all their feelings and desires are just "delusion"

Jennifer Gates and her husband Nayel Nassar (https://www.world-today-news.com/jennifer-gates-and-nayel-nassar-how-did-they-meet-the-love-story-of-the-daughter-of-bill-gates-nnda-nnlt-fama/)

Mark Zuckerberg and his wife Priscilla Chan (photo from Wikipedia)

Prince Harry and his wife Meghan Markle (photo from Wikipedia)

John Legend and his wife Chrissy Teigen (360dopes.com)

according to WEF, The Great Reset, and its promoter Yuval Noah Harari, and nothing is matter because they are just a bunch of molecules. They also should know that the NWO means to own nothing and be happy. All they need is to get their injections and implants in their brains.

Both Putin and Zelenskyy have the Jewish blood in their veins, they have no reason to fight. The difference between them is that they belong to different generations and that Zelenskyy is not a Jew Orthodox, he is a Jew who loves to dance wearing leather and stiletto (more satanic style, than Jewish), or even completely naked, and to play comedy for money and fame. There are a bunch of such videos of him circulating on internet.

One of the bestselling books today in the US is *The Satanic Bible* authored by Anton Szandor LaVey. It offers the core principles of the Church of Satan and is the foundation of philosophy of Satanism. This is considered the most important document today to influence contemporary Satanism.

Anton LaVey's (born Howard Stanton Levey, 1930-1997) father was Michael Joseph Levey from Chicago. His mother was a *Ukrainian*/Georgian woman Gertrude Augusta nee Coultron. And Zelenskyy, knowing it, could be very proud and influenced by the LaVey's Satanic philosophy.

Historian of Satanism Gareth J. Medway described LaVey as a "born showman." The academic scholars of Satanism Per Faxneld and Jesper Aagaard Peterson called LaVey as "the most iconic figure in the Satanic milieu." LaVey was an author, musician, Priest, and the founder of the Church

Zelenskyy flashing satanic signs (screenshot from video)

Zelenskyy dancing wearing stiletto (screenshot from video)

of Satan and the religion of Satanism. He authored several books: *The Satanic Bible, The Satanic Rituals, The Satanic Witch, The Devil's Notebook*, and *The Satan Speaks!*. Anton LaVey was born as Levey. In Russian, this word's [levey] pronunciation means "Left" (as an opposition to

Anton LaVey, 1992 (photo from Wikipedia)

the right). The accent should be made on the first letter 'e'. In Ukrainian, it also could be understood as the "Left" if the letter 'e' was pronounced as English 'ee', with the same accent, on the first letter 'e'.

Ukraine as a country found now itself in a complicated situation. Vladimir Zelenskyy's Advisor Alexey Arestovych is a very outspoken man. In one of his interviews he said: "The thing is that we are a f*cked up country. Plus we have f*cked up collective unconscious. The average Ukrainian, if it is possible to think in such categories at all, is an ideal victim of the information-semantic war. All connections in the brain are broken... suggestible. That is. Instead of a brain he has an ideal gas. An extremely instructive spectacle, I would say."

In another interview Arestovych said: "To vote for someone with the qualities of Zelenskyy - only complete r*tards could do that. I can not think of a better word, and at that, I am downplaying by 20 times the lexicon that would do it justice... . We are in a situation of the permanent war with Russia. How could a person be elected who says "war is not one of my priorities... ." You have to be an outright cretin, in a country at war, that is at war for at least 10 years and still to undergo several hot phases, to elect a person who says: "I do not like war but I will finish it." He [Zelenskyy] so unprofessional and stupid that he cannot understand that he cannot "finish" a war on his own. A war is either won or it is lost. There is no other way. What kind country do we live in if at least 50% of the voters have voted for someone who says: "So what with this war!" The situation is like this: say, you bring your mom to Emergency, and two doctors come out. One doctor said: I am a fat bastard, I make candies in my illegal factory, I am overweight, with diabetes, I take bribes, but I know how to treat people and I have 5 years of successful medical experience. Another doctor said, I am a honest person but I have no idea how to treat people. So what we have is 50% of voters [chose the 2ⁿᵈ one]!..".

Alexey Arestovych was interviewed a lot and these videos can be found everywhere in social media websites. He talks about Ukraine and Russia. He also explained how the Ukrainian government is manipulating the Ukrainian people's subconscious. There are the buttons to press, he said. First of all, trigger an alarm, then send a message that causes a feeling of guilt, these are a must. Then need to push on the "need for security." Them need to push on "belonging to a meaningful group." Then cheer a person up, encouraging him. Then need to lead him to a certain place. First you need to scare a person, then show the exist and form expectations for it, saying you will need to join here, do this, and everything will be fine. You need to say him: We are not afraid of anything anymore; Ukraine is well respected in the world; Ukrainians are the best soldiers, they fight to the end; we will not be deceived; the people have risen; the people will not allow...; those who join are cool. Then need to trigger the feeling of pride, self-praise: "There is simply no better soldier than Ukrainian, we winning better than anyone." And then what? Promise a reward: "If you do all that, it will be this." Exactly this technique was constantly used by Zelenskyy in his daily video addresses to the Ukrainians.

Alexey Arestovych working at gas station after he was removed from President Zelenskyy's office (screenshot from video uploaded on August 20, 2022 - https://www.bitchute.com/video/tKNctWUcvARp/)

According to sources, Alexey Arestovych was recently removed from his advisor's position because of his "politically incorrect", outspoken personality and interviews that went viral. The old official list of Zelenskyy's Advisors was updated in May of 2022 and the Arestovych's name is not there. There is a video appeared with him on August 20, 2022, working at the gas station. Arestovych said in this video that he was kicked out from the President's office and now has his new job at the gas station and it makes him very happy because not everyone can find a job these days in Ukraine.

This Ukraine-Russia conflict is a very bad thing. The regular people on both sides not need it. However, if it happened, somebody wanted and needed it very badly.

Recently Zelenskyy told a joke about this war: Two Jewish guys from the Ukrainian city Odesa meet up and having a dialog:

1st man - So what is going on, what is the situation, what are people saying?

2nd man - They are saying it's a war, war.

1st man - What war?

2nd man - Russia is fighting NATO.

1st man - Are you serious?

2nd man - Yes, yes. Russia is fighting NATO.

1st man - So, how is it going?

2nd man - Well.... . 70,000 of Russian soldiers are dead. The missile stockepile has almost been depleted. A lot of equipment is damaged, blown up.

1st man - And what about NATO?

2nd man - What NATO? NATO hasn't even arrive yet. (The audience laughing).

Zelenskyy telling a joke about war between Russia and NATO.

https://www.bitchute.com/video/OpjhIBxhrp8M/

In the meanwhile in the NYC's public places new digital ads appeared on the middle of November 2022 and later. Some ads were promoting the new bivalent covid-19 booster for New Yorkers 5 years and older, suggesting to get it as soon as possible. Another ad was suggesting to get the oral treatment if tested positive. Another ad was teasing those who were afraid of virus: "What if Covid-19 comes home for the holidays?" This ad was suggesting that Covid became their family member and will never leave them forever.

It felt like there is an oxidative stress in the country and worldwide.

Photo by Nadia Russ. New Covid-19 treatment promotion in New York, January 2, 2023

Photo by Nadia Russ. Ad promoting oral covid-19 treatment in NYC, December 25, 2022

Photo by Nadia Russ, the Covid-19 booster advertisement in NYC, November 2022

CHAPTER 6

PANDEMIC AMNESTY

In December 2021, a former Pfizer's vice president Dr.

Michael Yeadon filed a complaint with the International Criminal Court (ICC) on behalf of UK citizens against Boris Johnson and UK officials, Bill and Melinda Gates, chief executives of Big Pharma companies, WEF's chairman Klaus Schwab, and others for crimes against humanity, according lifesitenews.com.

The UK group, including an astrophysicist and a funeral director, additionally charged Dr. Anthony Fauci; Tedros Adhanom Ghebreyesus, director-general of the World Health Organization (WHO); June Raine, chief executive of Medicines and Healthcare products regulatory agency (MHRA); Dr. Radiv Shah, president of the Rockefeller Foundation; and Dr. Peter Daszak, president of EcoHealth Alliance, as "responsible for numerous violations of the Nuremberg Code ... war crimes and crimes of aggression" in the UK and other countries.

In the group's complaint filed December 6, they presented evidence that COVID-19 "vaccines" are in fact experimental gene therapies engineered with gain-of-function research from bat coronaviruses, arguing that these "vaccines" have caused massive death and injury and that the UK government has failed to investigate such reported deaths and injuries; that COVID case and death numbers have been artificially inflated; that face masks are harmful due to hypoxia, hypercapnia and other causes; and PCR tests are "completely unreliable" and "contain carcinogenic ethylene oxide," the lifesidenews.com wrote.

In August 2022, in Chicago, the health care workers won $10M settlement over hospitals' COVID vaccine mandate. NorthShore has to pay $10.3 million to employees who were denied religious exemptions. Founder and chairman of Liberty Counsel, Mat Staver was behind the settlement. He explained on "Fox & Friends" that NorthShore implemented a "jab or job" policy, meaning employees were required to get the vaccine or be terminated. NorthShore employees who were terminated or forced to resign would receive $25,000 and those who were forced to get the vaccine would receive $3,000 as part of the settlement, he said.

In the mid-October 2022, a federal judge has ordered Fauci and other Biden officials be deposed as part of a lawsuit against the Biden administration, alleging that the government colluded with social media companies to censor free speech related to the coronavirus and other controversial topics, the FoxNews said. According to a court order from the United States District Court for the Western District of Louisiana, U.S. District Judge Terry Doughty concluded that Fauci's high-profile public comments have made him a key figure in the lawsuit from the Republican attorneys general of Louisiana and Missouri who allege that "collusion" between the Biden administration and social media companies to censor coronavirus-related speech that could be damaging to the White House.

On October 31, 2022, *The Atlantic* published an article by Emily Oster *"Let's Declare A Pandemic Amnesty"*. She wrote: "... These precautions [social distancing] were totally misguided. ... Outdoor transmission was vanishingly rare. Our cloth masks made out of old bandanas wouldn't have done anything, anyway. ... there is an emerging (if not universal) consensus that schools in the U.S. were closed for too long: The health risks of in-school spread were relatively low, whereas the costs to students' well-being and educational progress were high. The latest figures on learning loss are alarming. ... Remember when the public-health community had to spend a lot of time and resources urging Americans not to inject themselves with bleach? That was bad. Misinformation was, and remains, a huge problem. But most errors were made by people who were working in earnest for the good of society. ..."

Despite all that above, Emily Oster suggested to "put these fights aside and declare a pandemic amnesty. We can leave out the willful purveyors of actual misinformation while forgiving the hard calls that people had no choice but to make with imperfect knowledge. ..."

How about the logic, Emily? How about the analytic abilities (that the higher education schools teach their students)? How about the regular common sense? There is always a choice, and we all still have the right to decide.

Emily Oster probably understood the stupidity of situation. She probably understood that she was participating in a foolish spectacle, directed by the agents of chaos "who were working in earnest for the good of society." And she wants forgive them. They will do it again.

By the way, who is Emily Oster, a school bus driver or a baby sitter? Emily Fair Oster is an American economist and author. She is currently the JJE Goldman Sachs University Professor of Economics and International and Public Affairs at Brown University, where she has taught since 2015. Her research interests span from development economics and health economics to research design and experimental methodology... . There are many more professors out there who have no logic nor analytic abilities or just hit by the S.S. or A.S.S..

November 23, 2022, I was given one dollar bill in some

Photo by Nadia Russ. One Dollar bill with handwritten message: "There is no virus, 5G is going to kill you"

NYC's store as a change. This is another way to pass the messages these days that are banned online. Actually why it should be only the scientists' privilege to know about radiation, the power of 5G, and about the radiation dangers. It should be the part of public education and knowledge.

Dr. Martin L. Pall, PhD and Professor Emeritus of Biochemistry and Basic Medical Sciences at Washington State University wrote in his report: "5G: Great risk for EU, U.S. and International Health! Compelling Evidence for Eight Distinct Types of Great Harm Caused by Electromagnetic Field (EMF) Exposures and the Mechanism that Causes Them": "Putting in tens of millions of 5G antennae without a single biological test of safety has got to be about the stupidest idea anyone has had in the history of the world."

The former President of Microsoft, Canada, Frank Clegg, released an educational video about the health and safety concerns of 5G and wireless technologies. He said that it is the fact that our Federal Health Regulatory Agencies have not put this type of technology through any type of safety testing before imposing it on the American, and global population. In fact, all of the research that's come out so far shows that it's not safe at all.

When it comes to radiation, the people have the long-term effects and the immediate symptoms, and some are more sensitive to it than others. In June 2020, the sciencedirect.com published an article authored by several scientists - Frank M.Clegg, Margaret Sears, Margaret Friesen Theodora Scarato, Rob Metzinger, Cindy Russell, Alex Stadtner, Anthony B. Miller. This article states that Radiofrequency radiation (RFR), used for wireless communications and "smart" building technologies, including the "Internet of Things," is increasing rapidly. ... Adverse biochemical and biological effects at commonly experienced RFR levels indicate that exposure guidelines for the U.S., Canada and other countries are inadequate to protect public health and the environment. ... 4.6. The common symptoms of Electromagnetic hypersensitivity (EHS) include headaches, cognitive difficulties, sleep problems, dizziness, depression, fatigue, skin rashes, tinnitus and *flu-like symptoms*. EHS also known as electrical sensitivity, electrohypersensitivity, idiopathic environmental intolerance, or microwave sickness. Adverse reactions to wireless devices range from mild and readily reversible to severe and disabling, and individuals must greatly reduce their exposures to sources. According to sciencedirect.com, the surveys conducted in several countries in 1998-2007 estimated that approximately 3%-13% or more of the population experience symptoms of EHS (electromagnetic hipersensitivity) when in contact with different types of radiation.

Screen shot from sciencedirect.com (https://www.sciencedirect.com/science/article/pii/S036013231 9305347)

In the meanwhile, another "scientific" website, called msn.com, published an AFP Fact Check article called "5G networks do not cause *'flu-like'* symptoms." In this article Claire Savage wrote: "Social media posts claim radiation from 5G technology makes people sick with flu-like symptoms. But US health authorities and independent experts say there is no evidence that wireless communication systems are harmful to humans."

AFP   AFP Fact Check

5G networks do not cause 'flu-like' symptoms

Story by Claire Savage, AFP USA • Feb 2

Social media posts claim radiation from 5G technology makes people sick with flu-like symptoms. But US health authorities and independent experts say there is no evidence that wireless communication systems are harmful to humans.

'Just a friendly reminder 5G radiation causes flu-like symptoms... #TheMoreYouKnow' a January 21, 2022 Facebook post says.

The "Fact-Check", screen shot from msn.com

Today, we have two types of science and scientists. First type is just the science and the scientists you can believe in/to, and the second type is the profit-based "science" and "scientists."

Chapter 7

I Would Not Be Able To Write This Book If...

I would not be able to write this book if I was a "hacked animal." I have my own opinion, vision, sense of humor, sarcasm, feelings, emotions. I am still a "delusional" individual. But if I was "hacked," then I would be a bunch of molecules with no ability to experience no feelings nor attachments. If I was a "hacked animal," I would write another book, a guide on how to practically achieve the state of happiness, while owning nothing, and how to enjoy life without privacy, helping WEF achieve their goal, that is so unpopular among the regular people. No wonder, the World Economic Forum deleted their tweet and denying that they ever said this: "You will have nothing and you will be happy!" However, the WayBackMachine restored it.

WEF's tweet restored by WayBackMachine: "Welcome to 2030. I own nothing, have no privacy, and life has never been better."

Klaus Schwab does not want the people had any privacy. Isn't this coincidence that he recently said that there would be a major cyber attack soon. According to the 2021 Cyber Threat Report by SonicWall, there has been a 62% increase in Ransomware since 2019. Ransomware is malicious software designed to encrypt files that prevent someone from using his computer. The cyber-criminals hold the data of governments, healthcare organizations, and companies across the world, sometimes demanding millions of dollars in payment. The organizations and individuals have to pay to hackers and cyber-criminals a ransom in exchange for access to their computers.

There was a page with this name in Wikipedia as well, till this morning... . It was very strange to see that this page "You Will Own Nothing and You Will Be Happy!" was

en.m.wikipedia.org/wiki/You_Will_Own_

≡ WIKIPEDIA   Q

You Will Own Nothing and You Will Be Happy!

Article   Talk

Sorry, this page was recently deleted (within the last 24 hours). The deletion, protection, and move log for the page are provided below for reference.

- 07:42, 26 November 2022 Liz (talk | contribs) deleted page You Will Own Nothing and You Will Be Happy! (Redirects from vandalistic page move) Tag: Twinkle

- 07:30, 26 November 2022 Adakiko (talk | contribs) moved page You Will Own Nothing and You Will Be Happy! to World Economic Forum over redirect (vandalism)

Look for **You Will Own Nothing and You Will Be Happy!** on one of Wikipedia's sister projects:

Wiktionary (dictionary)

Wikibooks (textbooks)

Page "You Will Own Nothing and You Will Be Happy" was deleted from Wikipedia on November 26, 2022 (Wikipedia's screen shot)

deleted from there two minutes before I visited Wikipedia with a purpose to take its screen shot for this book. They deleted it at 07:42 AM, November 26, 2022.

If I was a "hacked animal," I would write the Ten NWO commandments with exploration of their meaning because it is a very tricky thing. One of those commandments would be: Be generous, give everything to the folks like Klaus Schwab, Bill Gates, and Jeff Bezos, because they are the people in need.

If one thinks that the members of WEF who are working on a project of the 4th Industrial Revolution, the Great Reset, and "You Will Own Nothing and You Will Be Happy!" are the poor or middle class people, you are wrong. According Wikipedia, the foundation is funded by its 1,000 member companies, typically global enterprises with more than five billion dollars in turnover. These enterprises rank among the top companies within their industry. Membership is stratified by the level of engagement with forum activities, with the level of membership fees increasing as participation in meetings, projects, and initiatives increases. In 2011, an annual membership was $52,000 for an individual member, $263,000 for "Industry Partner" and $527,000 for "Strategic Partner." An admission fee costs $19,000 per person. In 2014, WEF increased the annual fees by 20%, bringing the cost for "Strategic Partner" from $523,000 to $628,000.

One of the WEF's board trustees is Mark Schneider. He is

Membership

The foundation is funded by its 1,000 member companies, typically global enterprises with more than five billion dollars in turnover (varying by industry and region). These enterprises rank among the top companies within their industry and/or country and play a leading role in shaping the future of their industry and/or region. Membership is stratified by the level of engagement with forum activities, with the level of membership fees increasing as participation in meetings, projects, and initiatives rises.[49] In 2011, an annual membership cost $52,000 for an individual member, $263,000 for "Industry Partner" and $527,000 for "Strategic Partner". An admission fee costs $19,000 per person.[50] In 2014, WEF raised annual fees by 20 percent, bringing the cost for "Strategic Partner" from CHF 500,000 ($523,000) to CHF 600,000 ($628,000).[51]

⌃ Activities

Annual meeting in Davos

WEF's Membership (screenshot from Wikipedia)

Board of trustees ✏️

The WEF is chaired by founder and executive chairman Professor Klaus Schwab and is guided by a board of trustees that is made up of leaders from business, politics, academia and civil society. In 2010 the board was composed of: Josef Ackermann, Peter Brabeck-Letmathe, Kofi Annan, Victor L. L. Chu, Tony Blair, Michael S. Dell, Niall FitzGerald, Susan Hockfield, Orit Gadiesh, Christine Lagarde, Carlos Ghosn, Maurice Lévy, Rajat Gupta, Indra Nooyi, Peter D. Sutherland, Ivan Pictet, Heizo Takenaka, Ernesto Zedillo Ponce de Leon, Joseph P. Schoendorf, H.M. Queen Rania Al Abdullah.[13] Members of the board of trustees (past or present) include: Mukesh Ambani, Marc Benioff, Peter Brabeck-Letmathe, Mark Carney, Laurence D. Fink, Chrystia Freeland, Orit Gadiesh, Fabiola Gianotti, Al Gore, Herman Gref, José Ángel Gurría, André Hoffmann, Christine Lagarde, Ursula von der Leyen, Jack Ma, Yo-Yo Ma, Peter Maurer, Luis Alberto Moreno, Muriel Pénicaud, H.M. Queen Rania Al Abdullah of the Hashemite Kingdom of Jordan, L. Rafael Reif, David M. Rubenstein, Mark Schneider, Klaus Schwab, Tharman Shanmugaratnam, Jim Hagemann Snabe, Feike Sijbesma, Heizo Takenaka, Zhu Min.[47][48]

WEF's board of past and present trustees (Wikipedia's screen shot made on November 26, 2022)

the **NESTLE company CEO and the active WEF's Agenda contributor. His resent DAVOS article of 01.16.2023 *"Consumers want sustainable options. What food producers, suppliers, and retailers can do now"* was published in the WEF's website. There, he is talking a lot about the climate change and global food system that**

 www.weforum.org/agenda/authors ≜ ⋮

World Economic Forum Annual Meeting Learn more >

WORLD
ECONOMIC
FORUM

Mark Schneider

Chief Executive Officer, Nestlé

Since January 2017, Chief Executive Officer, Nestlé. Joined the company in September 2016. 2003-16, Chief Executive Officer, Fresenius Group. Joined Fresenius in 2001 as Chief Financial Officer, Fresenius Medical Care. 1989-2001, held several senior executive positions with the Haniel Group, a privately held, diversified German multinational company. Graduate degree in Finance and Accounting and Doctoral degree in Business Administration, University of St. Gallen, Switzerland; MBA, Harvard University. Member of the WEF Board of Trustees; Member of the Board Consumer Goods Forum; Member European Roundtable for Industry.

Screen shot from the WEF's website

≡ INDIA TODAY   🅼🅰🅶 Magazine   📺 Live TV   🔍 Search

News / Business / Nestle's 'unhealthy' food portfolio controversy: ...

Nestle's 'unhealthy' food portfolio controversy: All you need to know

The world's largest packaged food and beverages company Nestle has found itself in a tough spot after an internal document suggested that 60 per cent of its mainstream product portfolio is "unhealthy". Here is all you need to know.

 India Today Web Desk 🐦
New Delhi, UPDATED: Jun 2, 2021 07:48 IST

"must quickly adapt to be more sustainable - while properly nourishing the growing global population." He also wrote there: "Transforming consumer demand is needed to help supercharge our collective ability to urgently get to net zero... ." In the meanwhile, his Nestle company is largely criticized because of more than 60% of its food and drinks could not be considered healthy under a recognized definition of health.

Recently, the Nestle was "nourishing the growing global population" with the added graphene oxide to the San Pellegrino water. Graphene Oxide was also found in vaccines despite it is a pathogen and dangerous for humans. The scientists at the Brown University found that the edges of graphene nanoparticles are very sharp and strong. They easily pierced through cell membranes in human lung, immune cells, and skin. They potentially can do serious damage in humans and animals.

Michael McKibben of the Leader Technologies and his group have investigated the history of the World Economic Forum's Klaus Schwab. In the audio posted in https://forbiddenknowledgetv.net/klaus-schwab-and-the-fourth-reich/, McKibben shares their shocking discoveries about Schwab, who was born in Nazi Germany and lived there with his father, whose family businesses were Nazi collaborators. During his life, Schwab has ingratiated himself to the Holy Roman Empire's royal houses. He did it to reach his main goal of consolidating Europe and now the world under the control of "the Gnomes of Basel" - the Swiss bankers.

Graphene (AlexanderAlUS, Wikipedia)

The WEF's leaders want to own everything they wish, but it seams like the rest should have by 2030 nothing. And the food quality expectations should be lowered as well. Even the Beatles' song "All You Need Is Love" is now outdated because feelings and emotions are "delusion," according to them. However, one allowed to get attached to kratom and marijuana, this is why the stores that sell these products are everywhere. All you need now is some distressed jeans with some sustainable t-shirt that you can get in a consignment store. Forget about fancy cars or cars in general. Walking and riding a bicycle is good enough. You also must be vaccinated according the WEF. If you do not like it, they still want get you. The scientists now put the mRNA vaccines into tobacco, lettuce, spinach and other plants.

The National Geographic July 7, 2021 in an article *"Your next vaccine could be grown in a tobacco plant"* wrote that Conventional vaccine manufacturing is costly and complex. This is why only some countries have the technology, funds, and human resources to make vaccines. Many countries have faced different challenges, such as the quality control in the race to manufacture, trying to distribute billions of COVID-19 vaccines.

Now scientists are changing their direction and are making something like a vaccine to COVID very fast. Now they can have tens of millions of vaccine available within next six months, the scientists at Cornell University said. They specialize in plant research and agricultural biotechnology and are hoping that this will open the floodgates for new developments in plant-made vaccine technology. They are hoping to have success in doing it.

The Hindustan Times wrote that scientists of the University of California, Riverside were studying the possibility of transforming edible plants into mRNA (Messenger RNA) technology vaccines against Covid-19. Associate professor in UC Riverside's department of botany and plant sciences, and the head of the research, Juan Pablo Giraldo said that the team was testing the plant-based vaccine approach with spinach and lettuce, with a long-term agenda of people growing these plants in their gardens. Farmers could also eventually grow entire fields of it.

These articles were published about 2 years ago and were not updated since then. We may eat now the plant-based vaccines and even do not know it? Nothing was said in those articles about the side effects and what if a person will get overdosed. If too much of sugar and salt or other stuff in food is not good for the human health and can lead to serious illnesses, what about the plant-based, edible vaccines overdose? Can people eat plant-based vaccine everyday as we used to eat salads?

The nature.com published an article *"How plants could Produce covid-19 vaccine,"* in which the CEO of Medicago company (Canada) said that their vaccines would be the first plant-derived ones for human use to reach the market, and they are the only plant-based manufacturing company that has been able to produce vaccines on a commercial scale. They have the capacity to produce millions of doses in their facilities in Durham, U.S. and Quebec City, Canada, where they are also building a new manufacturing facility. This is expected to open by 2023 and to expand their annual production capacity to 50 million doses of a quadrivalent seasonal flu vaccine or up to a billion doses of the COVID-19 vaccine.

Ripe tobacco leaves. Photo by Quang Nguyen Vinh (Photo free to use)

Can one grow Covid vaccines? Researchers say lettuce, spinach can replace the traditional mRNA shots

World News
Published on Sep 22, 2021 10:47 PM IST

The research team from University of California, Riverside, among others, are focusing on using chloroplasts that plants use to convert sunlight into energy, to produce edible plant-based mRNA Covid-19 vaccines.

The scientists said that they are testing the plant-based vaccine approach with spinach and lettuce, with a long-term agenda of people growing these plants in their gardens.

Written by Sharangee Dutta | Edited by Avik Roy, Hindustan Times, New Delhi

It's the end of 2021, which means more than two years of the world combatting the coronavirus disease (Covid-19) outbreak. While several anti-Covid vaccines have come up and vaccination is underway across the globe, they come with their set of challenges.

Aimed at addressing such challenges, scientists of the University of California, Riverside are currently studying the possibility of transforming edible plants into mRNA (Messenger RNA) technology vaccines against Covid-19.

Screen shot from Hindustan Times. Article about edible plant-based vaccine in lettuce and spinach

If I was a "hacked" animal, I would be not a human any more. I would be a red-blooded digital device (actually a blue-blooded, because I have the "royal," rh-negative blood type. Some call it the alien's blood type because it does not have the monkey's protein in it). I would have the cultural Marxist program installed in my brain, regularly updated during my sleep time with the new freaky stuff. This is the SIFI reality some people are dreaming about 24/7. By the way, according to Marxist doctrine, parents do not own their children... .

While I am still not a bunch of molecules, my computer is. It seams like it was hacked when I was writing this book. No, there was no malware problem.

I finished writing the whole book's text on November 11, 2022, and I saved it on my computer as usual. However, when I opened it next day, the last chapters were gone. It was a negative surprise because there was no book's duplicate. I had to start writing the missing chapters from the scratch, trying to recall everything. Honestly, the re-writing was not an exciting process. The thrill of creativity was lost.

Some unusual things happened to my computer. One day before the last chapters of my book gone, the Microsoft Windows of my computer was suddenly automatically updated. The next day I saw that AVG could not install their updates for unknown reason (first time in history of my use of this anti-virus program). Then, when next day the AVG installed their updates, it said that there was an issue with my computer operating system, offering to fix it. I decided to skip this fixing, not to make everything worse. I already knew about the operating system's issue because a few chapters of my book suddenly disappeared.

After this incident, I started saving the book's file not only on my computer but also on USB, in case the things will go wrong again. Yes, the things went wrong again a couple of times more, but not too dramatic. Only the last chapter's last paragraphs were missing in the book's file that I saved on my computer. But now they were easily restored because I had my book's copy saved on my USB as well. I am not sure if there were some minor changes in all chapters, I could not read the whole book daily.

***

The main idea of this book is to say Thank You to a great cardiologist doctor who 10 years ago successfully performed a procedure on my heart.

Before this procedure, I felt like I would die soon because my heart rate was often 300 beats a minute. I called a couple of times the Emergency and the medical personal at the trucks were making some injection into my arm's vein, normalizing my heart beat. However, the fast heartbeat events started happening too often, sometimes even twice a day. Once I called the Emergency and they brought me to a hospital, where cardiologist said that my problem could be fixed by a procedure on my heart. And I decided to get it.

When I was 24, I decided not to go to doctors if there was no emergency. By then, I already knew that the doctors were just the regular people and they were making mistakes too often to trust them. I still never take any medications as well, because the chemicals are treating one organ but they are destroying another. These are my 2 rules.

It was an emergency situation and I decided to give my life in the hands of God and the Cardiologist doctor, being a fatalist. Everything went perfect, the doctor was the best of its kind. Every year I was sending him to his medical office a *Thank You* card on Thanksgiving. This year I wanted to send him this book, but I could not make it by Thanksgiving because the half of chapters disappeared from my computer's file when it was almost ready to publish. I had to re-write all the missing text, starting from scratch. I feel that this my book's first version was read by some individuals, who were too in a hurry, just like I was in a hurry to publish it.

I did not disclose the doctor's

name because I am not sure if he'd want it. I do not know his political views. But I know that he fully dedicated himself to his profession and it probably gives him happiness and satisfaction. His life has tremendous meaning and cannot be underestimated by anyone because he spends his days to improve health of the common folks. This is awesome and unreal.

Some people spend days doing nothing or something to benefits only themselves; some people spend their lives to get more knowledge and pass it to others; some people live to ruin lives of others or to steal; some people dedicated their lives to make this world a better place; some people live doing crazy things while wearing the clever faces...· But there is a doctor, who dedicated his life to improve health to all, and do it not-stop· This requires significant knowledge and experience, it can be very stressful and not easy to do· But just think: he does it every day, excluding weekends· That's amazing·

CONCLUSION

This world is a mess because
many clueless people have their
ego increased to the size of our
Universe. They forgot that they
are just the wannabe Gods
humans, and they can be easily
destroyed by the nature, which
they are desperately trying to

control. The humans never will be gods, they never will know everything. The scientists love to experiment but they do it recklessly. Dreaming big is a great thing, but when making it reality, one should be in a healthy state of mind and very informed about all the consequences. We now live in a world when most of the authorities do not want to think about the consequences. They often do not want to be responsible for anything as well, however, they are expecting responsibility from other people, like doctors, for example. They want to know the consequences of their surgeries, procedures or treatments. Hopefully the common sense will dominate and our future will be better than the SIFI obsessed cultural Marxists draw in their narratives and preparation papers.

The Klaus Schwab's Great Reset and the 4th Industrial Revolution are not something exciting, they are not a sweet candy everyone would enjoy.

In one of his interviews Schwab said that China is the "role model" for the rest of the world.

If China was so good, Chinese people would not immigrate from there to the United States. There is nothing appealing to the American people about living in one-party communist country without freedoms and liberties, where the government oppresses its own citizens. It is obvious that the WEF's leader is not different than many totalitarian tyrants we know. He wants to install the one-world government that would control every person on this planet, exercising the WEF's totalitarian vision and looks like oppressive style, punishing those who disagree, just like in China.

Democracy and communism cannot co-exist. The American founding fathers developed a form of government suitable the human nature. The WEF and Schwab want re-make people to fit ideology they like and society they want to build for themselves, not for the people. In this society the people would be silenced, they would be the victims of propaganda, censorship, and lies. The American people should never give away their rights.

Follow these NeoPopRealist 10 Canons instead, which I created in 2004:

1. **Be beautiful;**
2. **Be creative and productive; never stop studying and learning;**
3. **Be peace-loving, positive-minded;**
4. **Do not accept communist philosophy;**
5. **Be free-minded, do the best you can to move the world to peace and harmony;**
6. **Be family oriented, self-disciplined;**
7. **Be free spirited. Follow your dreams, if they are not destructive, but constructive;**
8. **Believe in god. God is one, it is harmony and striving for perfection;**
9. **Be supportive to those who need you, be generous;**
10. **Create your life as a great adventurous story.**

REFERENCES

*Klaus Schwab: "God is dead" and the WEF is "acquiring divine powers"-
   https://www.youtube.com/watch?v=N2kLBJN5MIQ
   https://rumble.com/v1wy7me-klaus-schwab-god-is-dead-and-the-wef-is-acquiring-divine-powers.html
   https://yournews.com/2022/11/29/2462932/klaus-schwab-god-is-dead-and-the-wef-is-acquiring/

*Sacrifice in Carthage

   https://www.ox.ac.uk/news/2014-01-23-ancient-carthaginians-really-did-sacrifice-their-children

*Elon Musk wearing NWO jacket at Met Gala -

   https://www.investmentwatchblog.com/elon-musk-wears-new-world-order-jacket-to-the-met-gala-bloomberg-confirms-elon-is-a-young-global-leader-for-klaus-schwab-wef-great-reset

*Schwab talking about the brain implants -
   https://www.youtube.com/watch?v=64dKPF866mM

*Verses about Hell - https://dailyverses.net/hell

*Pfizer vaccine List #1 side effect - Chromosome 1p36 Deletion Syndrome - https://rarediseases.info.nih.gov/diseases/6082/chromosome-1p36-deletion-syndrome

*Pfizer vaccine List of side effects and adverse events - https://childrenshealthdefense.org/wp-content/uploads/pfizer-doc-5.3.6-postmarketing-experience.pdf#page=30

*Consumer Report - https://consumerreports.org/toxic-chemicals-substances/most-plastic-products-contain-potentially-toxic-chemicals

*Seven Types of Plastics: Their Toxicity - https://alansfactoryoutlet.com/7-types-of-plastics-their-toxicity-and-most-commonly-used-for

*Plastic and Heart Disease - https://jamesknellermd.com/plastic-and-heart-disease

*Why Do We Inhale Oxygen And Exhale Carbon Dioxide? - https://www.forbes.com/sites/quora/2017/02/28/why-do-we-inhale-oxygen-and-exhale-carbon-dioxide

*Inhaling pure oxygen could keep your brain younger for longer - https://www.popsci.com/story/health/anti-aging-treatment-oxygen

*Anti-Aging Oxygen Treatment Research - https://www.ncbi.nlm.nih.gov/books/NBK482485

*Benefits of Borjomi Mineral Water - https://en.happywellmag.com/761-borjomi-the-benefits-and-harm-of-mineral-water.html

*Lack Of Oxygen To The Heart Symptoms: Effects Of Low Oxygen Levels - https://www.tandurust.com/heart-health/lack-of-oxygen-heart-symptoms.html

*Heart Disease - https://www.mayoclinic.org/diseases-conditions/heart-disease/symptoms-causes/syc-20353118

*N.Y. Court Orders Rehiring Unvaccinated Workers - https://www.washingtontimes.com/news/2022/oct/26/ny-court-orders-rehiring-back-pay-for-fired-unvacc.

*Internet of Things - https://www.ibm.com/blogs/internet-of-things/what-is-the-iot

*The Fourth Industrial Revolution review – adapt to new technology or perish - https://www.theguardian.com/books/2017/jan/06/the-fourth-industrial-revolution-by-klaus-schwab-review

*Sustainable Development - http://un.org/documents/ga/res/42/ares42-187.htm

*Bioengineered Foods - https://encyclopedia.com/science/encyclopedias-almanacs-transcripts-and-maps/bioengineered-foods

*List of Bioengineered Foods (2022) - https://www.ams.usda.gov/rules-regulations/be/bioengineered-foods-list

*Premier of Alberta (CA) Fired Off on Klaus Schwab (WEF) - https://www.redvoicemedia.com/2022/10/alberta-premier-danielle-smith-fires-off-on-klaus-schwab-and-the-world-economic-forum

*Richard Sieger: List of the WEF Young Global Leaders From 1993-2021 and Covid YGL - https://plebeianresistance.substack.com/p/all-the-young-global-leaders-from?sr

*The WH website Archives - https://trumpwhitehouse.archives.gov/people/ivanka-trump

*Ivanka Trump at Davos WEF 2020 meeting - https://www.youtube.com/watch?v=mlpMomsOWxA

*Meet the Global Young Leaders Class 2022: https://www.younggloballeaders.org/community?class_year=2022&page=9&q=&region=&sector=&status=

*Klaus Schwab Talking About Penetration of Political Cabinets - https://rumble.com/vvdlhe-klaus-schwab-on-video-bragging-that-his-org-penetrated-prime-minister-trude.htm-

*WEF BioGenome Project: DNA database - https://www.weforum.org/press/2018/01/new-partnership-aims-to-sequence-genomes-of-all-life-on-earth-unlock-nature-s-value-tackle-bio-piracy-and-habitat-loss

*NHRC performing Genome sequencing - https://health.mil/News/Articles/2023/01/24/Genome-Sequencing-Assists-Research-at-Naval-Health-Research-Center?type=Publications

*US Coronavirus Deaths by Bleach Disinfectant Injection - https://www.indiatvnews.com/news/world/us-coronavirus-deaths-by-bleach-disinfectant-injection-major-rise-trump-covid-19-treatment-616708

*PayPal Misinformation Policy $2,500 Fee - https://townhall.com/tipsheet/leahbarkoukis/2022/10/28/paypalmisinformation-fee-n2615157

*Kratom - https://www.webmd.com/vitamins/ai/ingredientmono-1513/kratom

*Mark Zuckerberg in WEF - https://www.weforum.org/people/mark-zuckerberg

*Harari explains the WEF's Great Reset - https://rumble.com/vufrgx-tranhumanism-klaus-schwab-and-dr.-yuval-noah-harari-explain-the-great-reset.html

*Humans are Hackable Animals - https://americanfaith.com/human-beings-are-hackable-animals-free-will-is-over-world-economic-forum-doctor

*New Yorker about Harari's Book "Sapiens" - https://www.newyorker.com/magazine/2020/02/17/yuval-noah-harari-gives-the-really-big-picture

*Psychology.com About Harari's Sapiens - https://www.psychologytoday.com/us/blog/insights-more-meaningful-existence/202011/in-hararis-sapiens-meaning-life-is-just-delusion

*Quora - Was V. Putin Mother Jewish? - https://www.quora.com/Was-Vladimir-Putins-mother-Jewish?share=1

*Putin Invited the European Jews Immigrate to Russia - https://www.businessinsider.com/putin-calls-for-jews-to-emigrate-to-russia-2016-1?op=1

*Jewish Renaissance Under Putin - https://www.theyeshivaworld.com/news/featured/1824898/the-secret-of-putins-positive-relationship-with-jews.html

*Protest Ukrainian war - https://www.jpost.com/diaspora/article-716361

*Zelensky said to leave Donbass if you love Russia - https://anti-empire.com/zelensky-tells-russian-speakers-who-feel-themselves-russian-to-leave-donbass

*Pure Blood Was Important in the Nazi Germany - https://www.historylearningsite.co.uk/nazi-germany/blood-purity-and-nazi-germany

*Gene Modification - FDA - https://www.fda.gov/vaccines-blood-biologics/cellular-gene-therapy-products/what-gene-therapy

*Ukraine's MP Kira Rudik on Fox News: Me Fighting For NWO - https://www.independentsentinel.com/ukrainian-mp-says-theyre-fighting-for-the-new-world-order

*Daughter of Bill Gates Married Egyptian in Muslim Ceremony - https://english.alarabiya.net/life-style/entertainment/2021/10/17/Jennifer-Gates-marries-Egyptian-Nayel-Nassar-in-Muslim-ceremony-2-mln-wedding

*Mark Zuckerberg Wife Is Chinese-American - https://www.the-sun.com/tech/2582672/mark-zuckerberg-facebook-wife-priscilla-chan

*Jennifer Gates' Husband Is American-Arab - https://www.world-today-news.com/jennifer-gates-and-nayel-nassar-how-did-they-meet-the-love-story-of-the-daughter-of-bill-gates-nnda-nnlt-fama

*Multiracial Marriages On The Rise - https://www.brookings.edu/blog/the-avenue/2014/12/18/multiracial-marriage-on-the-rise

*Zelenskyy Advisor Arestovich: Ukraine Is the F*cked-Up Country - https://www.bitchute.com/video/DQbiHtWldLua

*Zelenskyy's Advisor Arestovych About Zelenskyy - https://www.bitchute.com/video/c4k9L2zR9RBc

*Current list of Zelenskyy's Advisors (Alexei Arestovych is not in it since May 2022) -

https://i.tyzhden.ua/novyny/08_2022/№1938%20(Голуб %20А_%20).pdf

*Zelenskyy Dancing Wearing Stiletto - https://rumble.com/vw7898-ukrainian-president-volodymyr-zelensky-in-a-gay-show-.html

*Mayor of Small Ukrainian City Konotop - ltranationalist - https://news.yahoo.com/ukrainian-mayor-heralded-by-many-is-ultranationalist-161819300.html

*Alexey Arestovich Explains How They Manipulate the Ukrainian People Subconsciousness - https://www.bitchute.com/video/mSiOb34LkuAR

*Alexey Arestovich said he was kicked out from Presidential Office. Video was posted online August 20, 2022 - https://www.bitchute.com/video/tKNctWUcvARp/

*Zelenskyy's joke about war between Russia and NATO- https://www.bitchute.com/video/OpjhIBxhrp8M/

*Health Care Workers Win $10M Settlement Over Vaccine Mandate -https://www.foxnews.com/media/health-care-workers-win-10m-settlement-hospitals-covid-vaccine-mandate-big-wakeup-call

*Fauci Sued - https://www.foxnews.com/politics/judge-rules-fauci-deposed-lawsuit-alleging-white-house-worked-with-big-tech-censor-speech

*A lawsuit filed in the International Criminal Court that alleges crimes against humanity (Fauci, Gates, Schwab, more) -

https://www.lifesitenews.com/news/big-pharma-execs-gates-fauci-uk-officials-charged-with-crimes-against-humanity-in-international-court

*Emily Oster proposed the Pandemic Amnesty - https://www.theatlantic.com/ideas/archive/2022/10/covid-response-forgiveness/671879

*Ex Vice President of Microsoft Explains How 5G Wireless Radiation Could Be A Huge Health Hazard - https://www.sgtreport.com/2019/10/ex-vice-president-of-microsoft-explains-how-5g-wireless-radiation-could-be-a-huge-health-hazard

*Martin Paul's Book Aboout Danger of 5G - https://www.emfacts.com/2018/08/martin-palls-book-on-5g-is-available-online

*Science to Protect Health and Environment - https://ehtrust.org

*The 5G Causes the Flu-Like Symptoms and Many Other, According to Scientists - https://www.sciencedirect.com/science/article/pii/S0360132319305347

*So-Called Fact Check - https://www.msn.com/en-us/health/medical/5g-networks-do-not-cause-flu-like-symptoms/ar-AATpkm2

*The Nestle CEO Mark Schneider is WEF's Agenda contributor - https://www.weforum.org/agenda/authors/mark-schneider

*Nestle CEO's Mark Schneider's article "Consumers want sustainable options. What food producers, suppliers, and retailers can do now" -

https://www.weforum.org/agenda/2023/01/consumer-power-net-zero-food-producer-retailer-davos23/

*Nestle unhealthy food controversy - https://www.indiatoday.in/business/story/nestle-s-unhealthy-food-portfolio-controversy-all-you-need-to-know-1809539-2021-06-01

*Graphene Oxide was found in Nestle's San Pellegrino water - https://rumble.com/v1oibl7-graphene-oxide-in-nestles-san-pellegrino-water.html

*Graphene Oxide, 5G and Covid-19 vaccines - https://radiationdangers.com/2022/01/11/the-connection-between-covid-5g-and-the-graphene-oxide-found-in-the-jabs-by-claire-edwards/

*Graphene Oxide dangerous for humans - https://newatlas.com/graphene-bad-for-environment-toxic-for-humans/31851/

*National Geographic: Your next vaccine could be grown in a tobacco plant - https://www.nationalgeographic.com/science/article/your-next-vaccine-could-be-grown-in-a-tobacco-plant

*Hindustan Times about plant-based eatable vaccines - https://www.hindustantimes.com/world-news/us-researchers-studying-if-lettuce-spinach-can-be-turned-into-covid-vaccines-101632330028954.html

*How plants could produce covid-19 vaccine - https://www.nature.com/articles/d42473-020-00253-2

*WayBackMachine - WEF: You'll Own Nothing and You Will Be Happy in 2030 - https://twitter.com/toastietruth/status/1533588778283159553

*Cyber attacks - https://www.privacyaffairs.com/cybersecurity-attacks-in-2021/

*ForbiddenKnowledge.net about Klaus Scnwab background - https://forbiddenknowledgetv.net/klaus-schwab-and-the-fourth-reich/

*According the Marxist Doctrine, Parents Do Not Own Their Children - http://www.vanguardnewsnetwork.com/2022/03/soviet-ideas-in-american-schools

The Interior of this book was completed January 29 2023, in the US. The minor edit was done on April 15, 2023 (Zelenskyy's joke was added).

NeoPopRealism Press
www.neopoprealism.org

Made in the USA
Middletown, DE
21 April 2023

28936060R00076